# Lincoln

# and Prevention of War

*Which 'Blundering Generation'?*
*What 'Irrepressible Conflict'?*

An Interpretation of the Lincolnian View

by

RALPH G. LINDSTROM

Lincoln Memorial University

*Harrogate, Tennessee*

1953

# Publisher's Foreword

A FRESH and moderate approach has been made by Ralph G. Lindstrom, a profound student of the political philosophy of Abraham Lincoln, in the conflicting viewpoint of two schools of thought among historians in evaluating the events which culminated in the Civil War of 1861-65. In a careful and thoughtful consideration of the issues which ultimately were decided by human conflict, Mr. Lindstrom rejects both the "revisionist" theory that the war was brought on by a "blundering generation," and the "irrepressible conflict" theory of the historians who assert that the tragedy of the war was inevitable.

In this thesis, Mr. Lindstrom attempts to show that Lincoln rejected the position of both schools of thought, and asserts that "the common people ... can solve any civic problem, under American federal state and national law processes, without violent arbitrament ... That is to say: Under the American constitutional and federal system, no conflict, in the sense of civic violence, is in itself irrepressible."

In these days of disorder and misunderstanding, Mr. Lindstrom has argued eloquently for a postulate of human conduct which should be pursued by world leaders in their effort to resolve the conflicting international issues which divide and confuse the peoples of the world. His position, based upon what he believes to be the Lincolnian view, he asserts "is the only safe remedy for what thunders back and forth between East and West today."

ROBERT L. KINCAID, *President*

*Lincoln Memorial University*
*Harrogate, Tennessee*

# Foreword

Two WORLD wars and the conflict in Korea, all happening within a generation, have led historians into new examinations of the inevitability or repressibility of war when antagonistic ideologies impinge on one another. Denied the long view essential to balanced judgment in the case of these recent conflicts, certain American historians have made our Civil War their laboratory. One group concludes that a "blundering generation" stumbled into a needless war. Another group argues that when controversy transcends constitutional, political, or economic bounds and becomes a question of right and wrong, compromise becomes impossible and armed conflict results. Thus moral questions are those most likely to be resolved by the most immoral means of war.

In this provocative little volume, Mr. Lindstrom, rejecting both the idea of a "blundering generation" and the rival conclusion of despair, finds a means to the peaceable coexistence of incompatible moral orders in a conception of the federal system such as Lincoln stood for. Examining the causes of the Civil War from a new vantage point, Mr. Lindstrom also suggests a solution of what is perhaps the major problem of our day—that of attaining effective world organization without sacrificing national sovereignty.

BENJAMIN P. THOMAS

*Springfield, Illinois*

# Lincoln
## and Prevention of War

### I

Is MAN doomed to exterminate himself in repeated and "irrepressible conflicts"? Must he, in endlessly weary repetition, work himself into one "log jam" after another, with no remedy but to dislodge the jam by violence?

Or, on the other hand, should man blithely and smugly dismiss past wars as merely the product of stupid, blundering generations?

Or are both views wrong? Can conflicts, under some workable system, be kept repressible and soluble without violence, during generations of average human beings? Can *homo sapiens* be saved from stupidly blundering either into barbarism or oblivion?

The task of this little work is analysis, in the light of Lincolnian logic, of these opposing views; with some exploration of the civic methods by which Lincoln felt sublimely certain:

a) that humanhood's "log jams" *can* be dislodged by and under safe and constitutional law-processes (even when highly explosive moral issues are involved), which seek out and dislodge the "key log," rather than resorting to senseless violence which simply blows everything apart;

b) that progress toward "man's vast future" can best be promoted and assured by a system of allocated law-power which preserves unity in diversity, and avoids centralized, unitary, far-removed and therefore despotic control of, and interference with, that self-government and internal self-control which permits, promotes and preserves fascinating variety in local custom, culture and control;

c) that man's greatest happiness can be found in creative achievement under *genuine* understanding of the greatest among self-evident civic truths—"that all men are created free and equal." This is to say that each man must, in some degree at least, appreciate that his equality with other men lies neither in division of things, nor in taking from another the fruit of his industry, nor in sharing scarcity; but rather it lies in ever-increasing measure of equality of opportunity and the "unfettered *start* (not guaranteed finish) in the race of life." Then disparity between men will exist only in the degree in which men vary in effort, initiative and so in individual achievement.

In entering into the debate between the revisionists of American history, who say the Civil War was solely the product of a stupid, blundering generation, and those who argue that the Civil War was an "irrepressible conflict" or log jam to be dislodged by violence, this writer feels as Lincoln said of himself at the opening of his great 1854 speech at Peoria: "Fools rush in where angels fear to tread."

Then Lincoln went on:

"At the hazard of being thought one of the fools . . . I rush in, I take that bull by the horns."

And then he proceeded to demolish the Douglas "popular sovereignty" excuse for nullifying the Missouri Compromise in the name of "the sacred right of self-government." Lincoln observed that Senators in Washington had not fairly met Douglas on that issue.

The writer is a lawyer, not an historian. Nevertheless he follows Lincoln's example and, at the hazard of being "thought one of the fools," he takes hold of the quarrel of the 1940's and 1950's between the "revisionist" school of Civil War historians, and the "irrepressible conflict" school. Abraham Lincoln prospectively rejected both propositions, as does this writer, in the light of what Lincoln has said and written.

The "revisionist" school would re-write history to show that the Civil War was occasioned solely by a "blundering generation"; that slavery would soon have ended, anyway, as an uneconomic labor system.

The "irrepressible conflict" school consists of those who feel that occasionally mankind works itself into a political or civic "log jam" which can only be dislodged by an explosion, the explosion being an "irrepressible conflict." Since modern thermo-nuclear violence would dislodge much more than the log jam, the question or controversy would seem due for review.

A great Civil War historian, Allan Nevins, at Springfield in the fall of 1950, gave what Carl Sandburg, the next day, standing on the beautiful bluffs at restored New Salem, called "the best biography ever done of Stephen A. Douglas."[1]

Indian Summer in Illinois is a time for reflective consideration and careful thinking. It was in October, 1854, that Lincoln set a standard of such thinking at Peoria. Nevins and Sandburg intimately know this standard. Theirs is a rare understanding of the greatest federalist of them all—Abraham Lincoln.

It was altogether "fitting and proper," and no less timely, that Nevins should make that Springfield speech. His *Ordeal of the Union* and *Emergence of Lincoln* (Scribners) are two of the most scholarly of the studies of the people and events of the 1840's and 1850's. But the timeliness lay in the raging conflict between "revisionist" and "irrepressible conflict" schools of Civil War historians. And Nevins himself had only shortly before been wrongly accused of "revisionist" views, as we shall shortly see.

The Nevins speech, and that erroneous charge of "revisionism" against him, prompt this analysis of the "revisionist-irrepressible conflict" debate. One need accept neither view. There is another position, the federal view, and the purpose here is to present it.

---

[1] *Journal of the Illinois State Historical Society,* vol. XLIII (1950) p. 13 (hereafter cited as "Journal").

# II

## *The Federal Way*

IT MAY well be true to say that the stupidity and blundering of Lincoln's generation induced the departure from our federal constitutional system which, in turn, brought on the Civil War. But, if true, it is not for that reason also true that such blundering stupidity exceeds, or even equals, that of our present generation. We, also, have too far lost sight of federal constitutionalism.

*Any* conflict which is repressible and avoidable, in the logic of events and of law, can be made irrepressible by rejecting that logic of events. The mature conclusion and intuitive sense of the unpretentious group called, by Lincoln, "the common people," free and healed of, or better still saved from, the foul spirit of politically-purposed hysteria, can solve any civic problem, under American federal state and national law processes, without violent arbitrament. Put differently, that is to say: under the American constitutional and federal system, no conflict, in the sense of civil violence, is in itself irrepressible.

But what kind of a man was this Douglas of whom Nevins spoke? Until Nevins, or some historian with equal ability, shall write a full biography, one can do no better than read "Stephen A. Douglas: His Weakness and Greatness" by Allan Nevins in the December, 1949, *Journal of the Illinois State Historical Society.*

There Nevins discussed the view of Albert J. Beveridge, who accepts the validity of Douglas' "popular sovereignty." [2]

Nevins shows Douglas as a man who ran the whole gamut (even as late as 1860, and when a candidate for the Presidency) from a loose, boisterous, half-drunk campaigner, to great nobility.[3] In 1861

---

[2] *Journal,* Vol. XLII (1949) p. 386 (subsequent citations to this Nevins speech will be merely by page number in the footnote).

[3] Albert J. Beveridge, *Life of Lincoln,* 1809-1858 (Houghton Mifflin).

(April 25), as the defeated candidate, he supported Lincoln in a series of speeches, including a great speech at Springfield, where he eloquently urged men to save the Union.[4] Nevins makes us see this strange combination of weakness and strength in Douglas, first yielding to the proslavery extremists in the Kansas-Nebraska bill, and then defying them in the battle against the Lecompton Constitution which President Buchanan sought to force upon Kansas.[5]

Douglas was a "brilliant improviser . . . all his life." The judge who gave him a license to practice law said: "He is no lawyer. . . . "[6] "No man was ever quicker to take practical advantage of any situation, and few leaders have been more careless of the long look ahead." "He was as deficient in general ideas of an abstract kind as he was fertile in working devices."

It is understandable why Beveridge should like the Douglas idea of "popular sovereignty." Douglas was the author of laws for admission of Florida, Texas, Iowa, Wisconsin, and California to statehood, and of territorial laws for Oregon, Minnesota, Washington, Utah, New Mexico, Kansas, and Nebraska.[7] It was the sort of "manifest destiny" which Beveridge, when he was United States Senator, was one day to urge as basis for American imperial dominance in Asia and the Far East.[8]

"[Douglas'] concept of the Union was Jacksonian, while Lincoln's concept was Websterian . . . Douglas saw the Union [utilizing] . . . its strong arm to annex new territory for the swarming American Millions. Lincoln's idea of the Union embraced this and a good deal more. He . . . thrilled to the Union with . . . a passionate attachment to the republic as a whole . . . If the Union died, liberty died with it. They were 'one and inseparable.' "[9]

Thus, as Nevins proceeded in his speech, and as we go on in this discussion, to question Douglas and his improvisations, it was not, and is not, to question Douglas' own sense of integrity and sincerity. It is rather to question his capacity to take the "long look ahead." Douglas, in the 1850's, was merely a politician. Lincoln had become a political-statesman by 1854. Douglas saw only the short

---

[4] *Journal* cited, p. 387.
[5] Idem, p. 389.
[6] Idem, p. 391.
[7] Beveridge, Vol. II, p. 169.
[8] *Americans of Today and Tomorrow*, Altemus Company (1903). Ch. V.
[9] *Journal*, cited, p. 395.

range interest, and improvised for it without regard for ultimate consequences. Lincoln had come to see liberty under law as a long-range, universal principle which only the federal plan could preserve and extend.

Douglas, like Beveridge, was interested primarily in America as an empire. Lincoln was deeply interested in the entire family of man, with the United States taking spiritual leadership to preserve a system of law which shall one day insure universal liberty under a federal plan which alone can preserve unity in diversity.

Nevins rightly characterizes Douglas' Kansas-Nebraska Bill as "the unhappiest Pandora's box in history."[10] The Bill showed "Douglas' tendency to gain an immediate practical end by impulsive improvisation."[11] How well Nevins sums it all up:

"As *first* introduced (the Nebraska Bill) merely stated that new Nebraska Territory should ultimately be admitted as a state with or without slavery as its constitution might prescribe. *Then* it was amended to declare that, pending statehood, all questions pertaining to slavery should be left to the people. *Finally* it was again amended to include an explicit repeal of the Missouri Compromise restriction against slavery. Plainly, Douglas had leaped into the situation without real forethought about his ultimate goal. He had taken a *first* hurried step. *Then* a group of Southerners pushed him to a *second, more drastic* step. *Then* still another Southerner, Dixon of Kentucky, pushed him to *the third step*. His first leap had seemed safe enough, but its momentum carried him forward to ground that quaked with danger. (Emphasis added.)

"In all American history no more fateful piece of headlong improvisation can be found than this Kansas-Nebraska bill. Before he introduced it the slavery question had been settled for every inch of American territory. Under the compromises of 1820 and 1850 not a rod of ground was in dispute. This impetuous measure opened up two mightly quarrels. . . .

" . . . In a sense, Douglas spent his final years battling for his one broad, hazy principle—the principle that the people who go to dwell in a given area should determine its institutions. It was not so sound a principle as Lincoln's doctrine that national morality and

---

[10] *Journal*, cited, p. 401.
[11] Idem, p. 403.

national health called for the containment of slavery within its existing bounds." [12]

Yes, it is good that, while Nevins shows the weaknesses of Douglas and his impulsive mistake in the Kansas-Nebraska bill, he also points out the sober courage of this man in the fall of 1860.

Seeing that Lincoln would be elected President, Douglas went into the South to urge the people to submit to the Federal Government under Lincoln. He declared at Raleigh: "I would hang every man higher than Haman who would attempt to resist by force the execution of any provision of the Constitution which our fathers made and bequeathed to us."

It is good thus to see and think of Douglas in the last year of his life as finally transcending reckless improvisation to manifest the brave statesmanship of which he was capable. If Douglas had only in earlier life been able to wed the Lincolnian type of deliberate and careful thought with the quick and impulsive brilliance he possessed, he would have become one of the country's greatest statesmen.

---

[12] Idem, pp. 403-4.

# III

## *Irrepressible Conflict School*

ANOTHER great historian, Arthur Schlesinger, Jr., writes for the "irrepressible conflict" school.[13] He quotes and criticizes this Nevins' statement:[14]

"The primary task of statesmanship in this era, was to furnish a workable adjustment between the two sections, while offering strong inducements to the southern people to regard their labor system not as static but evolutionary, and equal persuasions to the northern people to assume a helpful rather than scolding attitude."

But Schlesinger probably could not then have read what Nevins said in Springfield that same month, but which was not in print until December. And to say that a workable adjustment was available is not to be a revisionist of Civil War history.

There *was* a "workable adjustment" available. The understanding and application of the federal plan, as Lincoln urged, was that workable adjustment. Perhaps, if the North had not first practiced nullification in refusing to support a fugitive slave law, as required by the Federal Constitution, the Unionists in the South might not have come to final support of slavery expansionists (first relatively few in number). These slavery expansionists asserted external sovereignty for the slave institution of their states. They argued that slave state law accompanied them into free states and territories. Had there been no interference with their peculiar institution *within* slave states, Southern Unionists might have joined in the view that slavery in the territories was within the internal sovereignty delegated to the United States over territories. It was so exercised in the Missouri Compromise, and with many Southern congressmen so voting. Nevins is historically and federally realistic, not

---

[13] October, 1949, *Partisan Review*, "The Causes of the Civil War."

[14] Ibid, 970.

revisionistic, when he says there was available a "workable adjustment between the two sections."

Schlesinger has greater justification for classifying Avery O. Craven as an adherent of the "revisionist" view of Civil War history. His *The Repressible Conflict* (1939) and *The Coming of the Civil War* (1942) are repeatedly referred to by Schlesinger. He quotes Craven as describing "the growing sense of sectional differences as 'an artificial creation of inflamed minds.' " [15] He also shows Craven as critical alike of John Calhoun and John Quincy Adams, of Wilmot (for his Proviso) and Douglas (for the repeal clause in the Kansas-Nebraska Act as "the afterthought of a mere handful of politicians"), of Chase, and also of the dissenting judges in the Dred Scott decision. Schlesinger charges Craven with being an apologist for slavery,[16] but in a footnote states that Professor Craven "modified his earlier extreme position" in his article "The Civil War and the Democratic Process." [17]

Yet Professor Craven's latest volume, *The Growth of Southern Nationalism* (Louisiana State University Press) adheres to the view that when issues are stated in principles, they cannot be compromised; and then the breakdown of the democratic process is inevitable. Would he turn from American representative democracy?

To return to Schlesinger: Professor Craven did argue in the *Quarterly* that there was a "breakdown of the democratic process in 1860." He suggests a "dilemma inherent in (the) implications" of the Declaration of Independence, on the one hand, and the Constitution of the United States on the other hand. He calls the Declaration "a rather labored affair," and says it is based on Isaac Newton and a concept of "higher law" which made "civil disobedience" a virtue—this, after quoting from the Declaration. In such views Craven does revise both history and federal civics into misconceptions. If he had made a clear statement of sovereignty and, on such premise, had based his historical views, he certainly would not have derided the declaration that certain "truths (are) ... self-evident." [18]

---

[15] *Partisan Review*, Oct. 1949. (Subsequent citations to this article will be merely *Partisan Review* with the page number.)

[16] *Partisan Review*, pp. 972-3.

[17] *Abraham Lincoln Quarterly*, June, 1947. (Subsequent citations to the Craven article will be made by citing Craven, with page number.)

[18] Craven, pp. 270-2.

Certainly it *is* self-evident "that all men are created equal" [they were given dominion over all the earth (Gen. 1:26), thus "endowed by their Creator."] This is to say that all men have equality in the right to seek and achieve happiness and prosperity. Therefore "governments are instituted among men, deriving their just powers from the consent of the governed." This is to say that sovereignty is internal self-control (whether in individual person or individual unit of government) and that imposition of alien and external control is not sovereignty, but anarchy. Consequently, men have the right to abolish misconceptions of government or governments in so far as it or they assert the right externally to impose alien will, without consent of the governed, under the pretense of "external sovereignty." When men revolt against external force, they merely reject anarchy masquerading under the solecism of "external sovereignty," which is neither law nor government.

When the choice is between 1) civic enslavement, or 2) government under law with consent of the governed, the Declaration says it is the innate, God-given right of men either 1) to alter the "*form* of government" which asserts the "external sovereignty" to impose alien will against the consent of the governed, or 2) to abolish the "*form*" which has *ceased to be* "government." Then men necessarily "institute new government" to "effect their safety and happiness." This is the essence of our Declaration of Independence.

# IV

## *Constitutional Consistency*

CRAVEN likewise misconceives the Federal Constitution as definitely as he misconceives the Declaration of Independence. How could that be? How could so fine an historian go so wrong? Perhaps it is proof again that every human makes mistakes and proves his bigness in a willingness to correct them.

But here is what we read at page 274 of his *Quarterly* article:

"Now here were two fundamental American documents,—the one framed to establish a government; the other framed to *justify revolution* against a government. The one intended to set up a more perfect Union and protect the fixed rights of men against the whims and passions of those who might destroy; the other intended to stress those abstract rights of mankind which grow and expand and change almost constantly,—rights of human beings ultimately resting on the 'higher law' that knows no fixed bounds save those of a just and moral universe.

"As a pure abstraction such differences were of no consequence, but what if some fine day one group of Americans should appeal to one of these documents to prove and protect *its* rights and interests, and another group of Americans should appeal to the other document to prove and protect a conflicting set of rights and interests? What if the law of the land as embodied in the Constitution should not remain in accord with some men's reason and conscience, and they should appeal to the Declaration of Independence and the higher law it justifies? Then, perhaps, the Constitution would be burned and the phrases of the Declaration would be dismissed as mere 'glittering generalities,'—as doctrine both 'false and foolish.' "

Well, let's go back to the Declaration for a moment and again refer to its basis in what is, perhaps, the earliest declaration of sovereign power. Man was given "dominion over all the earth"

(Gen. 1:26). He was nowhere, by divine decree, or even by civic logic, given domination over other men. Certainly there is nothing of "pure abstraction" in such supremacy in self-control.

But the great Declaration set up no vague "higher law" to justify civil disobedience. The Lincoln mind, from Indiana youth to full-flowered maturity at Gettysburg and the Second Inaugural, never was even tempted by the Seward-Chase-Sumner-Phillips-Garrison doctrine of "higher law" and, consequently, justified civil disobedience. Why not?

The only higher, or highest, civic law Abraham Lincoln knew or accepted in the area of human government was the forever fact that sovereignty is internal self-control, and ever must be, and must ever be limited to internal self-control, whether of individual man or individual unit of government of whatever size. No interference with or encroachment upon that internal self-control can ever be justified by ANY abstract principle of morals or "higher law." Moral reform within an individual, or within an individual unit of government, is and ever must be the product of internal self-control. Destruction even of slavery, the most patent and blatant civic and moral evil of Lincoln's time, should not have been sought through abolition or "higher law" violation of the internal right of slave states to be even morally wrong in their domestic affairs. Conversely, this moral wrong of slavery (while not to be externally interfered with because within the internal sovereignty of slave states) should not be permitted to expand, and for two reasons: 1) that it was morally wrong, and the "suffer it to be so now" tolerance of it should not be enlarged to a claim that it was right, and even divinely ordained; and 2) that the expansion of this moral wrong to other states and territories of the United States would involve external imposition of the institution by means of assertion by slave states of external force and sovereignty for slave laws beyond the limits of the slave states. Such "divine ordination" and external imposition would destroy our national federal plan and result in retrogression into the anarchy which existed between the states before the federal union.

Before federal union, each state claimed "external sovereignty" as well as the true sovereignty of internal self-control.

There was nothing abstract in Lincoln's position. There is nothing abstract in the "higher law" or "highest law" of civics, which is sovereignty within, but never external to, an area of government.

(Even today, many in California, and elsewhere in the Union, detest the legalized gambling of Nevada, and hold it heinous moral wrong; but Californians do not for a moment entertain any "higher law" basis for direct interference, either by our larger California population and power, or through the federal power, with that internal affair of Nevada.)

Also, it *is* "self-evident" that men *are* "created equal" with "inalienable" right to "life, liberty, and the *pursuit* of happiness." Why overlook that word "pursuit"? Even God, himself, the ultimate Source and repository of all sovereignty, does not prevent man from accepting the most horrible misconceptions and from embracing the most wicked immorality. He gives man "life (and) liberty" with which to *pursue* happiness. How he pursues happiness is a matter of man's internal self-control unless, and until, he impinges on the rights of others. Internally he will pay the price, but civil law intervenes only to protect others from his wrong.

The people who came from England and other lands to settle America desired internal self-control and government with representation and consent of the governed. They saw that, with the evolution in civics from Magna Charta on, the human civil law came increasingly to be patterned on the divine. It was only when Parliament and a King denied local, internal control, and imposed taxation without representation, that the Colonists commenced effort to "alter" what was becoming only a "*form* of government" which denied innate rights of representation. Failing that, they abolished, as related to the Colonists, this "government" which had become only a form.

It must be repeated: the highest human pattern of the divine, as relates to government, is the "inalienable" right of the individual, and of groups of people organized as government, to use life and liberty in "the pursuit of happiness" in an area of internal sovereignty or self-control.

Whenever the peoples (that means groups of individuals) of separate sovereign units feel that some matter which has previously been within the *internal* control of their respective, but separate sovereign units, would better be delegated to some over-all unit of government (as the question of slavery outside the slave states and in United States territories; also abolition of slavery by the XIIIth Amendment; likewise, commerce physically within a state, but as part of an interstate movement of people or property from state to state, were delegated to our federal government), then, they, as *one people* for national matters, but comprised *of separate peoples* of separate states for local matters, can take such subjects from their separate governments and delegate jurisdiction over them to an over-all government strictly limited in power to such matters.

Thus, this delegated jurisdiction still remains true sovereignty—sovereignty internal to the newly created over-all area of legal jurisdiction.

It was this very delegation of limited authority over given subjects, by the *"people of the United States"* (comprised of the peoples of thirteen states) to the federal government which these same people (not the States) created by our Federal Constitution, which has made the United States the most peacefully prosperous people in the history of the world.

# V

## *Ballots, not Bullets*

WE HAVE always had, throughout our history, innumerable conflicts "of basic values, or moral standards; of the most fundamental things in the national make-up," but one must remind Professor Craven that these have not even tended to "create a situation where discussion would be utterly useless and compromise impossible." [19] True, we sometimes have rather wild campaigns; but we have, with only the one exception of the Civil War, reached decision with ballots, not bullets.

It was *not* the immorality of slavery *within* the slave states; it was not the "conflict of basic values, or moral standards" between the free state people and the slave state people which made "discussion . . . utterly useless and compromise impossible."

It was failure to keep that discussion and compromise within and under the federal plan; it was nullification, North and South; it was secession, North and South; it was the external interference of abolitionists from free states with the internal institution of slavery in slave states; it was the claim of external sovereignty by slavery expansionists for the slave laws of their states, by which they would take slavery, as of right, into new areas and against the will of the residents of other states and territories; it was Northern nullification of the Fugitive Slave Laws and Southern threats of secession—all these (not any abstract moral question) which created "a situation where discussion (became) useless and compromise impossible."

But the principle of the Declaration is not, and was *not*, "a pure abstraction." It was *not* a question whether even the moral wrong of slavery was "in accord with some men's reason and conscience." It was a specific matter of federal law and plan of government,

---

[19] Cited *Journal*, pp. 274-5.

which was flaunted, by abolitionists in the North and secessionists and slavery expansionists in the South. Lincoln urged that slavery be quarantined within, but protected within, the domestic area of slave state law, until the *people of those states* saw that it was not only morally, but also economically, wise to eliminate it. Thus, Lincoln pleaded that we return the question to the "course of ultimate extinction" principle where the Constitutional Fathers placed it, and which was wholly consistent with the federal plan of government. This solution was reached by them because the constitution was written when discussion was kept useful and compromise possible under the federal plan and approach.

The *repressible* conflict, by retrogression in civics to the anarchy of external interference to impose alien will in matters of local self-control, became the *irrepressible* conflict. Any generation which reverses the logic of civic events is a stupid generation. Lincoln's generation was stupid for failing, in apt time, to heed what Lincoln said.

The writer's generation has been twice stupid. It could have commenced building federal law solely for world affairs. It could have said to national socialism and communism alike: "We despise and detest the internal slavery implicit in your systems, yet we shall not interfere in your internal affairs. We shall, however, sterilize your systems of revolutionary expansionism in imposition of them on unwilling peoples. We shall neutralize in your systems the anarchy called 'external sovereignty.'"

The result of confining such systems to the area where the people have voluntarily accepted them, or allowed themselves to be victimized by them, will be ultimate abolition of the systems from within, because only during their expanding phase do they survive. Thus, we eliminate the only real hazard such systems have for other peoples—revolutionary expansionism. No slave economy can fairly compete with free enterprise.

Free peoples need not fear a genuine test between a free way of life and initiative, and a slave way of life and regimentation. Slavery is not voluntarily chosen by people who have known genuine freedom. If dictatorships decline to come in and be governed and tested by such a federal law system, then free peoples must go ahead without them. We did just that in the United States when the Federal Constitution was made effective, as to the states which ratified, when any nine of the thirteen should ratify. As a matter of fact, New York and Virginia, the two largest states, were the tenth and eleventh to ratify.

In Part IV of his paper, Craven seems to go all the way to the position that the Civil War was merely a matter of economic conflict, and resulted from "national pride" with "swaggering demands for territorial expansion that passed under the guise of 'Manifest Destiny.' " If Professor Craven means that swaggering territorial expansionism misled Douglas into repeal of the Missouri Compromise, we agree. Because he too, was a disciple of "Manifest Destiny," Beveridge thought better of the Douglas position than the view of Lincoln.[20]

But, if Craven implies that our federal experiment in democratic government suffered "complete breakdown" and "complete abandonment" because "issues dealing with right and wrong and issues that have to do with the fundamental structure of society do not lend themselves to the democratic process," [21] we must respectfully, but vehemently, disagree. There is, and was in the 1850's, a way to deal with such issues, and safely. It is a way as American as the United States Federal Constitution, based, in turn, on the great Declaration of self-evident truths.

The abolitionists in the North; the Calhoun-Rhett external sovereignty (claiming that, when a citizen of South Carolina entered into a United States territory with his slave, it was "the ingress of his sovereign, the State") and secessionist doctrines; the destruction of the "course of ultimate extinction" of slavery embodied in the Ordinance of 1787 and the destruction of the Missouri Compromise by repeal, and the *Dred Scott* decision—all these show no breakdown of our federal democratic process. They show a failure to use, a departure from, our federal process. They are proof that failure to *understand* and *use*, and be *governed*, and *blessed* by the federal governmental process brings disaster.

This federal "course of ultimate extinction" process of compromise as to slavery meant that, if the right and wrong of slavery had been left to, but confined within, the slave states and in "the fundamental structure of (our federal) society . . . the democratic process" *would* have solved the question without breakdown.

Since God, himself, leaves the highest moral questions, in human

---

[20] P. 277 ff.
[21] P. 291.

affairs, to internal solution of individuals and groups of people; so our federal plan can, and does, leave internal matters for internal solution—even where highest moral issues are involved. It is not logical to call failure to *use* and *apply* a plan a *breakdown* of the plan itself.

Professor Craven, like Douglas, gets in deeper and deeper:

"The experiment in democratic government, at least up to 1848, seemed to be succeeding. It was, however, a purely political success, —one which accepted the claims of sectionalism and established ways as equal to those of a crowding, driving modern national-ism. . . . " [22]

This simply is not correct. We repeat, until 1848 (really 1847, when Calhoun in the Senate and Rhett in the House announced their doctrine of external sovereignty for South Carolina and its slave institution) the hazards of sectionalism were obviated. The Calhoun–Rhett speeches were more or less fantastic assertion until repeal of the Missouri Compromise. The ultimate result of that re-peal, and of the Dred Scott decision, was to make territories before statehood the battleground, in an area of anarchy, for the conflict-ing moral views of free state people, who considered slavery an evil, and slave state people who had commenced to argue that it was divinely ordained and good. Again it must be said: This was not breakdown, but a failure to *understand* and *use* the federal demo-cratic process.

---

[22] P. 279.

# VI

## *No Breakdown Inevitable*

P ART V of the Craven article refers to the general agreement of
historians (which he apparently would revise) that the "complete breakdown" and "ultimate abandonment" of the democratic process "was due to the institution of slavery." Again we must
disagree. It was *not* "due to the institution of slavery" itself; but it
*was* due to taking that question from the place where it safely rested
under the federal plan, within, but confined to, the slave states
(where the Constitutional Fathers left it for "ultimate extinction"
by enlightened internal action of slave state people), and expanding it into the territories before statehood. Such violation of the
federal plan made each territory an area of anarchy between slave
state and free state people.

Again and again one must repeat that the unhappy Pandora box
of the Kansas-Nebraska Bill was not *breakdown* of, but *failure to
use*, the federal democratic process.

Mr. Craven twits the historians:

"To read some of their writings one would think that 'the dark
cloud of slavery' appeared suddenly out of nowhere in the years
around 1850; that, for the first time men had become conscious of
its evils and launched a great moral crusade against an institution
that had no place in the modern world."

We agree with the implication that "the dark cloud of slavery"
did *not* suddenly appear out of nowhere. But the dark cloud of
putting an explosive moral issue over slavery out of an area of legal
jurisdiction and into an area of anarchy between slave and free
states *did* suddenly appear "out of nowhere" in the Rhett-Calhoun
Congressional assertions of 1847. Douglas and the Supreme Court
gave it storm-cloud proportions by destroying the ultimate extinction process of gradual extirpation through voluntary state
action.

Clearly, Professor Craven is right when he says: [23]

"In the territorial struggle, Southerners had insisted both on the constitutional obligation of Congress to protect slavery in the territories and on the unconstitutionality of Congressional interference with slavery in the territories."

Certainly, that puts the proposition and the inconsistency of the Southerners' contentions concisely and clearly. The converse should, in fairness, be stated:

"In the slavery struggle, Northern abolitionists insisted both on the constitutional obligation of Congress to regulate slavery in the territories and on the 'higher law' right to nullify Congressional enactments required by the Fugitive Slave requirement of the Constitution."

Craven's continued argument is confused and confusing. True, Southerners talked incessantly of rights under the Constitution "like the repeated call of a whip-poor-will." True, Garrison and his friends would burn the Constitution; and the other school in the North turned to the Declaration of Independence and assumed (but wrongly) that there they found a "higher law" doctrine.

Craven puts Lincoln, and the Declaration of Independence, in wrong company and context. True, Lincoln pointed to "the eternal conflict between right and wrong" and his hope "that in due time the weights would be lifted from the shoulders of all men." This was no assertion of "higher law" to nullify the federal plan. It was *advocacy* of the federal plan whereby men achieve solutions in high moral issues without sectional conflict over them. Abraham Lincoln ever treated the Declaration and Constitution as one consistent whole, two parts of one federal plan—a Declaration of fundamental truth and right implemented by the Constitution. It is a startling conclusion, and wrong, very wrong, which Craven reaches: [24]

"What stands out in this story is the simple fact that issues dealing with right and wrong and issues that have to do with the fundamental structure of society do not lend themselves to the democratic process."

Misconception and cynicism are twins when he quotes Carl

---

[23] P. 283.
[24] P. 291.

Becker approvingly in his statement that "discussion proves efficient, only 'when there is nothing of profound importance to discuss.'"

Disagreement with Professor Craven does not preclude gratitude to him for bringing into sharp focus what is probably the most important question for consideration in the world to-day. That question is: how can conflicting systems, such as communism and true democracy, safely co-exist in a world shrunk to the size of a fist? There *is* a way. It is the federal way. And the genius of the federal plan is that it keeps such issues from becoming sectional conflicts. It keeps them from explosive proportions through revolutionary expansionism, either through infiltration and subversion, or through direct force subjugation.

True it is, as Craven quotes Seward, that "a moral question, transcending the too narrow creeds of parties" had arisen in the 1850's. True it may be, as Craven concludes his article, that what Seward "did not understand was that parties based on 'natural justice' and 'human liberty' might threaten vested interests and create conditions in which calm and rational discussion, tolerance of differences, and compromise, would be impossible." But Professor Craven missed the "if" which could have prevented the Civil War, World Wars I and II, and is the only means of preventing World War III, and probable consequent retrogression to barbarism.

Moral questions, natural justice, and human liberty—"issues dealing with right and wrong"—have never (excepting in our Civil War) brought "complete breakdown and ultimate abandonment of (the democratic) process;" and then only because we failed to stay under the American federal plan.

Wisconsin has gone the whole cycle from left to right; California (particularly Southern California) sometimes has toyed with many forms of "crackpotism"; Huey Long took Louisiana through a dictatorship that was not far from complete suspension of republican or representative government; Nevada lives on gambling and divorce—and all these involve moral questions, natural justice, and concepts of human liberty.

Such problems are neither geographic nor sectional. The only way they *could* become geographic or sectional would be if some of the states should seek to expand their systems and, by "external sovereignty" impose them upon adjoining areas; or if, conversely, states which disapproved, say, of legalized gambling or divorce mills in Nevada, interfered in the internal affairs of that state to force their elimination against the internal will of Nevada.

All of this is to say that internal control and exclusion of alien or external control, leaving over-all affairs to over-all law which, in turn, is confined in jurisdiction to over-all affairs; confining jurisdiction of each lesser-than-whole area of government to its internal affairs, but preserving its internal control as supreme—this is the way, under the federal plan, in which "moral questions," matters of "natural justice" and "human liberty" can be kept within non-explosive proportions and conciliatory compromise, pending ultimate solution.

If fascism and naziism had been so confined, there would not have been World War II; and, if communism is now so confined, free peoples can be assured that World War III need not, and will not, occur. If a people of a country choose, or allow themselves to be victimized into a given system of government, they should be allowed to test it for themselves on its merits. Equally, however, they should be *forced* to test it *within the confines* of their internal, domestic life, and not be permitted to force it, by alleged external sovereignty, on other peoples who do not wish or choose the system. This is what is meant by sterilizing systems such as communism of "revolutionary expansionism"—a phrase for which I give credit to Raymond Swing.

The federal system simply forces people who internally accept any system to let the system stand or fall on the basis of internally testing and demonstrating its workability—or failure. Communism confined is communism's collapse.

Professor Schlesinger, in his *Partisan Review* article, also charges that the late Professor James G. Randall has emerged "as the leader of a triumphant new school of self-styled 'revisionists.' "[25] He also says Randall denies what Schlesinger calls "the traditional assumption of the inevitability of the (Civil) War and (has) boldly advanced the thesis that a 'blundering generation' transformed a 're-pressible conflict' into a 'needless war.' " These criticisms reflect misconceptions of what Randall has written.

In so far as Professor Randall's splendid volumes—*Lincoln the President: Springfield to Gettysburg* (1945), *Lincoln and the South*

---

[25] P. 969.

(1946), and *Lincoln the Liberal Statesman* (1947)—indicate a view that there was not much choice between the Lincoln views and the Douglas contentions, this writer cannot agree. Neither can this writer accept Dr. Randall's description of the Kansas-Nebraska Act as "a law intended to subordinate the slavery question and hold it in proper proportion." This is said with deepest admiration and gratitude for the invaluable work of Dr. Randall on the Lincoln and Civil War themes.

But is it fair to assume, as Professor Schlesinger does, that Dr. Randall thinks "that history teaches us that evil will be 'outmoded' by progress and that politics consequently does not impose on us the necessity for decision and for struggle;" that Dr. Randall does not "understand that sometimes there is no escape from the implacabilities of moral decision;" or that Dr. Randall expects us to be "consoled by sentimental theories about the needlessness of the Civil War into regarding our own struggles against evil as needless"?

Dr. Randall never assumed that there was no moral decision involved in slavery. Southern men at the Constitutional Convention, and many other Southerners thereafter, also believed slavery to be a moral wrong. But isn't there a touch of the Garrison-Phillips attitude in the assumption that, since Randall says the Civil War *was a repressible* conflict needlessly *made irrepressible* by a stupid, blundering generation, he is thereby self-convicted of a dulled moral sense, seeking "escape from the implacabilities of moral decision" and "regarding our own struggles against evil as needless"? Such assumptions are not fair to Dr. Randall or his writings.

This is not to say that the Randall writings have fully embraced the thesis of this work. Yet, one finds no Randall assumption that *this* generation, for example, is not blundering as badly as the generation of Abraham Lincoln.

Dr. Schlesinger quotes from Dr. Randall:[26]

"To suppose that the Union could not have been continued or slavery outmoded without the war and without the concomitants of war is hardly an enlightened assumption," and rather sarcastically calls it "a touching afterglow of the admirable nineteenth-century faith in the full rationality and perfectibility of man; the faith that errors of the world would all in time be 'outmoded.'"

---

[26] P. 979.

Perhaps Dr. Randall would not have accepted what here follows. In any event, this writer does not presume to attribute the view to him. But, to answer Schlesinger, one may observe that the Constitutional Fathers had faith that the Union could be continued when they placed slavery in "course of ultimate extinction," expecting its ultimate extinction without war.

Why, then, did we have Civil War? War came because some Northerners, in the smugness of "Garrisonian" and "Phillipsian" abolitionism, would set aside the Constitutional and federal plan for ultimate extinction of slavery. Instead, they asserted that righteousness was somewhat of a sectional thing, with exclusive residence in the North, and must be imposed from without on the slave states. This was met by a counter-absurdity from South Carolina, describing slavery as a divinely ordained institution which slave owners could export for external application anywhere and everywhere, as of right, and under the slave laws of their own states.

Even when Douglas and the Supreme Court, in Dred Scott, gave this Calhoun-Rhett absurdity legislative and judicial blessing, Abraham Lincoln, the most consistent federalist of his day, still decried all claims that morality, righteousness, civic logic, and constitutional respect were sectional things with primary residence in the North. He pleaded that the question of slavery be returned to the "ultimate extinction" arrangement, by control under federal law, so that people could once again rest in the feeling that it *was* safely, within our federal system, in "course of ultimate extinction."

Lincoln hated slavery more intelligently than Garrison or Phillips. He loved the Union more. He was neither immoral, unmoral, nor amoral; nor did he accuse the South of being so. He had no "complacencies about human nature," but he certainly did not assume, as Schlesinger does to-day,[27] that "man occasionally works himself into a log-jam; and that the jam must be burst by violence." The violence of atomic-hydrogen explosions will burst more than "the jam."

No, Lincoln knew that, "when social conflicts embody great moral issues," the way to keep the family of man from a log-jam to be burst by the violence of inevitable war is to recognize that "faith in the full rationality and perfectibility" of human beings is to

---

[27] *Partisan Review*, p. 980.

"overrate man's (human) capacity."[28] Therefore, Lincoln saw that the Federal Union established a safe law basis for *homo sapiens*. How then would Lincoln answer Schlesinger? Would he not say (we paraphrase):

Avoid self-righteous "intra-meddling," even with moral issues in the internal affairs of other individuals or governments. When you make a federal compact, consistently keep it. If you would avoid external interference with *your* affairs, do not externally interfere with the internal affairs of *others*, not even on moral issues. Where you have over-all law, let it be supreme in over-all affairs, but never seek to apply it to the internal affairs of even the smallest and weakest unit within the whole. Equally be alert against assertion of externally imposed will called external sovereignty by any person or state on any other person or state, for that is anarchy. Thus, may the irrationality and imperfectibility of human beings be kept within safe limits and not become sectional conflict as step-by-step, and in the evolution of safely-confined self-control, and without periodic reversion to the barbarism of war, *homo sapiens* may go on to achieve "man's vast future."

Is the foregoing a fair interpretation of the Lincolnian view? It rejects the "revisionist" view in so far as that view, in turn, rejects the moral issues involved in slavery. It rejects also the inevitable and "irrepressible conflict" view, in so far as that view assumes that moral issues bring into play a "higher law" in connection with "great moral dilemmas" which only the violence of war can solve because man is not "capable of transcending the limitations of his being."[29] It is the federal law solution, without war, wherein moral issues may be safely solved in an area of internal control without developing competitive claims to sectional self-righteousness and corollary claims of moral idiocy elsewhere. It is the only safe remedy for what thunders back and forth between East and West to-day.

---

[28] Idem, 979-80.
[29] Idem, 981.